The Complex PTSD and Dissociation Handbook

A Guide to Overcoming Childhood Trauma, Dissociative Symptoms, and Finding a Path to Recovery and Thriving

Linda Horton

Table of Contents

PART I: UNDERSTANDING CHILDHOOD TRAUMA AND COMPLEX PTSD

Chapter 1

Introduction to Childhood Trauma

Childhood trauma casts a profound shadow that often extends far beyond the formative years, shaping an individual's worldview, relationships, and mental well-being. At its core, childhood trauma refers to adverse experiences that occur during the developmental years, leaving lasting imprints on a person's psyche. These traumatic events encompass a spectrum of experiences, each with its unique implications for a child's emotional and psychological development.

1.1 Definition and Types of Childhood Trauma

Defining childhood trauma involves recognizing a range of distressing experiences that can significantly impact a child's sense of safety and security. Physical abuse, emotional neglect, sexual exploitation, and witnessing domestic violence are among the types of trauma that can befall a child. The effects of trauma can be immediate or may manifest later in life, influencing mental health, interpersonal relationships, and overall quality of life.

One prevalent form of childhood trauma is emotional abuse, which often occurs insidiously and leaves invisible scars. Verbal degradation, constant criticism, and humiliation can erode a child's self-esteem and contribute to long-lasting emotional distress. Physical abuse, another stark reality, not only inflicts immediate harm but also leaves a lasting impression on a child's perception of themselves and others.

Sexual abuse, a deeply disturbing form of childhood trauma, shatters a child's innocence and trust. The betrayal of trust by someone in a position of authority can lead to profound emotional turmoil, often impacting adult relationships and intimacy. Neglect, whether physical or emotional, is equally detrimental, as it deprives a child of the fundamental nurturing required for healthy development.

Understanding the nuances of childhood trauma involves acknowledging the intersectionality of these experiences. Children from marginalized communities may face additional challenges, as systemic factors compound the impact of trauma. For instance, exposure to community violence or discrimination can exacerbate the psychological toll of childhood trauma.

1.2 Impact of Childhood Trauma on Development

The repercussions of childhood trauma are far-reaching, extending into various facets of a person's life, and understanding these impacts is crucial for effective intervention and support. Developmental psychologists assert that early experiences shape the architecture of the brain, influencing emotional regulation, cognitive functioning, and interpersonal skills.

In the realm of emotional development, childhood trauma can disrupt the formation of secure attachments. The foundational relationships established in early years serve as templates for future connections. Trauma-induced disruptions in these relationships can contribute to difficulties in forming healthy bonds and trusting others, often echoing into adulthood.

Cognitive development is not spared from the clutches of childhood trauma. Exposure to chronic stress, common in traumatic situations, can impair cognitive functions, including memory, attention, and problem-solving skills. This cognitive dysregulation may manifest as difficulties in academic settings, hindering educational attainment and perpetuating cycles of disadvantage.

The impact of childhood trauma on social development is profound, influencing a child's ability to navigate relationships and societal expectations. Trauma survivors may exhibit maladaptive social behaviors, such as aggression or withdrawal, as coping mechanisms developed in response to early adverse experiences. These behaviors can pose challenges in forming meaningful connections and participating in social activities.

Moreover, childhood trauma is intricately linked to mental health outcomes. Trauma survivors are at an increased risk of developing mental health conditions, including but not limited to depression, anxiety disorders, and post-traumatic stress disorder (PTSD). The enduring psychological effects of childhood trauma underscore the importance of early intervention and therapeutic support.

Chapter 2

Unraveling the Layers of Complex PTSD

Complex Post-Traumatic Stress Disorder (C-PTSD) delves beyond the traditional understanding of PTSD, acknowledging the intricate layers of trauma that can persist over an extended period. While PTSD typically stems from a single traumatic incident, C-PTSD arises from prolonged exposure to trauma, often involving interpersonal violence, neglect, or captivity.

2.1 Differentiating PTSD and Complex PTSD

Post-Traumatic Stress Disorder (PTSD) has long been recognized as a psychological response to a traumatic event, characterized by symptoms such as intrusive memories, flashbacks, and hyperarousal. However, Complex PTSD extends the scope of trauma, emphasizing the impact of prolonged, interpersonal trauma. The key differentiator lies in the duration and nature of the traumatic exposure.

PTSD often results from a discrete event, such as combat, sexual assault, or a serious accident. The trauma is time-limited, and symptoms may emerge in response to reminders or triggers associated with the traumatic incident. In contrast, Complex PTSD arises from chronic, repetitive trauma, frequently occurring in interpersonal relationships where trust and safety are violated over an extended period.

A crucial element in differentiating the two is the concept of developmental trauma. C-PTSD recognizes the significance of early life trauma, especially when it occurs within the context of caregiving relationships. Children subjected to ongoing abuse, neglect, or betrayal may develop complex symptoms that go beyond the diagnostic criteria for PTSD. Understanding the developmental trajectory of trauma is pivotal in distinguishing between these two disorders.

Moreover, the impact of Complex PTSD is not limited to the classic symptoms of PTSD. While flashbacks and nightmares may be present, individuals with C-PTSD often grapple with pervasive issues in self-concept, interpersonal relationships, and emotional regulation. The nuanced presentation of symptoms in C-PTSD requires a comprehensive assessment that considers the broader effects of prolonged trauma.

2.2 Recognizing Symptoms of Complex PTSD

Recognizing the symptoms of Complex PTSD involves acknowledging the multifaceted nature of the disorder. The diagnostic criteria for C-PTSD include disturbances in self-organization, affect dysregulation, and interpersonal difficulties. These manifestations highlight the intricate ways in which chronic trauma can shape an individual's psychological landscape.

A core aspect of C-PTSD is the disruption in a person's sense of self. Individuals may struggle with a fragmented self-identity, feeling disconnected from their core being. This identity disturbance often stems from the pervasive nature of the trauma, impacting the development of a coherent and stable self-concept. Therapeutic interventions for C-PTSD often involve addressing these identity disturbances to facilitate a more integrated sense of self.

Affect dysregulation is another hallmark of Complex PTSD. The emotional rollercoaster experienced by individuals with C-PTSD includes intense and unpredictable emotional responses. From overwhelming sadness to explosive anger, these emotional fluctuations can be challenging to manage. Therapeutic strategies focus on enhancing emotional regulation skills, empowering individuals to navigate the complexities of their emotional landscape.

Interpersonal difficulties in C-PTSD are profound, reflecting the erosion of trust and safety in relationships. Survivors may oscillate between intense fear of abandonment and an aversion to closeness. Establishing and maintaining healthy connections becomes a significant challenge, as the relational templates shaped by early trauma often perpetuate dysfunctional patterns. Therapeutic interventions for C-PTSD prioritize rebuilding trust, fostering healthy boundaries, and enhancing communication skills.

The recognition of Complex PTSD requires a nuanced understanding of how trauma extends beyond the traditional boundaries of PTSD. While both disorders share common elements, C-PTSD encompasses a broader spectrum of symptoms, reflecting the enduring impact of chronic trauma on an individual's sense of self and relationships. As we unravel the layers of Complex PTSD, it becomes evident that a holistic and trauma-informed approach is essential for accurate diagnosis and effective therapeutic interventions.

Chapter 3

The Role of Dissociation in Trauma

Dissociation, a complex psychological process, serves as a coping mechanism in response to overwhelming trauma.

3.1   Understanding Dissociative Symptoms

Dissociation encompasses a spectrum of experiences that involve a disconnection between thoughts, identity, consciousness, and memory. It is a defense mechanism that the mind employs to shield itself from the intensity of traumatic experiences. Understanding dissociative symptoms is paramount in recognizing the profound impact of trauma on an individual's mental and emotional well-being.

One common manifestation of dissociation is depersonalization, where individuals feel detached from their own bodies or sense a distortion in their perception of reality. It creates an eerie feeling of being an observer to one's own life, as if watching events unfold from a distance. This detachment often serves as a protective mechanism, allowing individuals to endure traumatic experiences without the full weight of emotional distress.

Derealization, another facet of dissociation, involves a distorted perception of the external world. The surroundings may appear surreal or unfamiliar, contributing to a sense of unreality. This altered perception serves as a buffer against the harshness of traumatic events, creating a psychological distance from the distressing reality.

Amnesia, a hallmark of dissociation, can manifest as gaps in memory surrounding traumatic incidents. The mind, in an effort to shield itself from the overwhelming emotions associated with trauma, may selectively block or compartmentalize memories. These memory gaps can contribute to a fragmented sense of self and hinder the processing of the traumatic experience.

Identity confusion is a profound consequence of dissociation, where individuals may experience a blurred or shifting sense of self. The continuity of identity becomes disrupted, leading to internal conflicts about one's core beliefs, values, and personal history. This fragmentation of identity is intricately linked to the enduring impact of trauma on the foundational aspects of an individual's psyche.

Furthermore, dissociation often involves the presence of distinct personality states, a phenomenon known as Dissociative Identity Disorder (DID). In DID, formerly known as multiple personality disorder, different identities or "alters" emerge as a way for the mind to compartmentalize and manage traumatic experiences. Each alter may have its unique characteristics, memories, and ways of interacting with the world.

3.2 How Dissociation Manifests in Daily Life

Dissociation is not confined to traumatic moments; its influence extends into the fabric of daily life, shaping how individuals navigate the world around them. Understanding how dissociation manifests in daily life is crucial for both individuals experiencing dissociative symptoms and those providing support and care.

In interpersonal relationships, dissociation can present challenges, as individuals may struggle to connect emotionally or feel fully present with loved ones. The protective barriers created by dissociation, while adaptive in traumatic situations, may hinder the formation of meaningful bonds. Loved ones may find it perplexing when someone they care about seems emotionally distant or struggles to recall shared experiences.

Occupational functioning can also be significantly impacted by dissociative symptoms. Difficulties with concentration, memory lapses, and episodes of dissociation during work tasks can undermine productivity and job performance. Individuals may grapple with the dual challenge of managing the demands of daily responsibilities while contending with the intrusive nature of dissociation.

Education is another domain where the impact of dissociation is palpable. For students contending with dissociative symptoms, challenges in concentration and memory retrieval may impede learning and academic achievement. The academic environment, with its inherent stressors, can serve as a trigger for dissociative episodes, further complicating the educational experience.

Dissociation's influence on self-care is profound. Individuals experiencing dissociative symptoms may struggle to engage in activities that promote well-being, such as proper nutrition, exercise, and sleep. The disconnection from one's body and emotions can create a sense of apathy or detachment, hindering the motivation to prioritize self-care.

Driving and other routine activities also pose potential risks when dissociation manifests unexpectedly. A dissociative episode while driving, for example, can jeopardize safety. Understanding these daily challenges is essential for developing strategies to enhance safety and well-being for those managing dissociative symptoms.

PART II: NAVIGATING THE RECOVERY JOURNEY

Chapter 4

Building a Foundation for Recovery

Recovery from trauma is a nuanced and complex journey, requiring a solid foundation that encompasses emotional support, understanding, and self-care.

4.1 Establishing a Safe Support System

At the core of building a foundation for recovery lies the establishment of a safe and nurturing support system. Trauma survivors often grapple with the aftermath of their experiences, and the presence of a reliable support network becomes a cornerstone in their healing journey.

The first step in this process involves identifying individuals who can provide genuine support and understanding. This may include close friends, family members, or even support groups comprised of individuals who have experienced similar traumas. The key is to create a network where survivors feel seen, heard, and validated, fostering an environment conducive to healing.

Therapeutic support is a crucial component of a safe system. Mental health professionals, including psychologists, counselors, or therapists specializing in trauma, play an instrumental role in guiding survivors through the recovery process. These professionals provide a structured and confidential space for survivors to explore and process their experiences, offering valuable insights and coping mechanisms.

Building a safe support system also involves setting boundaries with individuals who may inadvertently contribute to retraumatization. Educating those within the support network about the specific needs and triggers of the survivor fosters a more empathetic and informed environment. This collaborative approach ensures that the support system aligns with the survivor's unique journey towards healing.

In some cases, survivors may find solace in connecting with peer support groups. These groups offer a shared space for individuals who have experienced similar traumas to exchange insights, coping strategies, and mutual encouragement. The sense of community cultivated within these groups can be a powerful antidote to the isolation that trauma often imposes.

Cultivating a safe support system goes beyond emotional support; practical assistance can be equally impactful.

Helping survivors with daily tasks, such as childcare, grocery shopping, or transportation, can alleviate additional stressors, allowing them to focus on their recovery. This collaborative effort reinforces the sense of belonging and interconnectedness within the support system.

The establishment of a safe support system is an ongoing process that adapts to the evolving needs of the survivor. Regular communication, transparency, and a commitment to mutual growth contribute to the resilience of this foundation for recovery.

4.2 Self-Care Practices for Trauma Survivors

Self-care is a vital component of the recovery journey for trauma survivors, encompassing intentional practices that nurture physical, emotional, and psychological well-being. Tailoring self-care practices to address the unique needs and challenges of trauma survivors is a delicate yet empowering process.

Physical self-care involves attending to the body's needs, acknowledging the interconnection between physical and emotional well-being. Regular exercise, even in gentle forms such as yoga or walking, contributes to stress reduction and promotes a sense of grounding. Adequate sleep is equally essential, as trauma often disrupts sleep patterns. Creating a consistent and calming bedtime routine can support survivors in reclaiming a restful night's sleep.

Nutritional self-care focuses on nourishing the body with wholesome and balanced meals. Trauma can impact appetite and eating habits, and survivors may find solace in rediscovering a positive relationship with food. Seeking guidance from nutrition professionals or incorporating mindful eating practices can foster a healthier approach to nutrition.

Emotional self-care involves nurturing one's emotional landscape through various practices. Mindfulness and meditation, for example, offer survivors tools to anchor themselves in the present moment and manage overwhelming emotions. Journaling is another effective outlet, providing a safe space for survivors to express their thoughts and feelings, fostering self-reflection and insight.

Creativity can be a powerful avenue for emotional expression and healing. Engaging in art, music, or other creative pursuits allows survivors to tap into their inner resources and channel emotions in a constructive way. Creative self-expression can serve as a non-verbal outlet for processing trauma and reclaiming a sense of agency.

Psychological self-care emphasizes therapeutic interventions that support survivors in understanding and navigating their mental health. Cognitive-Behavioral Therapy (CBT), Eye Movement Desensitization and Reprocessing (EMDR), and other trauma-focused therapies provide structured frameworks for addressing the impact of trauma on thought patterns and behaviors. These therapeutic modalities empower survivors to reframe negative beliefs and build resilience.

Spiritual self-care acknowledges the importance of connecting with one's sense of purpose and meaning. For some survivors, this may involve engaging in religious or spiritual practices, while others may find solace in nature, mindfulness, or volunteer work. Cultivating a sense of spiritual well-being provides a broader perspective that transcends the immediate challenges of trauma.

Balancing self-care practices requires a compassionate and adaptive approach. Each survivor's journey is unique, and self-care evolves as individuals progress in their recovery. Regular reassessment of self-care strategies, guided by the survivor's changing needs and insights, ensures that these practices remain aligned with the ongoing process of healing.

Chapter 5

Therapeutic Approaches for Complex PTSD

The journey toward healing from Complex Post-Traumatic Stress Disorder (C-PTSD) demands specialized therapeutic interventions that address the intricate layers of trauma's impact.

5.1 Cognitive-Behavioral Therapy (CBT)

Cognitive-Behavioral Therapy (CBT) has emerged as a foundational therapeutic approach in the treatment of various mental health disorders, including Complex PTSD. CBT operates on the premise that thoughts, feelings, and behaviors are interconnected, and modifying negative thought patterns can lead to changes in emotional and behavioral responses.

In the context of Complex PTSD, CBT aims to identify and challenge distorted cognitions related to the traumatic experiences. This process involves exploring maladaptive beliefs about oneself, others, and the world. Survivors often internalize negative beliefs stemming from the trauma, such as a profound sense of guilt or an exaggerated perception of danger. CBT provides a structured framework to examine and reframe these beliefs, fostering a more balanced and realistic perspective.

Behavioral interventions within CBT focus on modifying patterns of avoidance and withdrawal that are common in C-PTSD. Exposure therapy, a component of CBT, helps survivors confront and process traumatic memories in a controlled and supportive environment. Gradual exposure to distressing memories allows individuals to build resilience and diminish the emotional charge associated with traumatic experiences.

CBT also incorporates skills-building components to enhance emotional regulation. Survivors of C-PTSD often grapple with intense and fluctuating emotions, and CBT equips individuals with practical strategies to manage overwhelming feelings. This may involve learning relaxation techniques, mindfulness practices, and assertiveness skills.

A crucial element of CBT for C-PTSD is addressing core beliefs related to safety, trust, and self-worth. Therapists work collaboratively with survivors to challenge and restructure these beliefs, fostering a sense of empowerment and agency. By dismantling negative thought patterns, CBT facilitates the development of a more adaptive and resilient mindset.

The structured and goal-oriented nature of CBT aligns well with the needs of individuals navigating the complexities of Complex PTSD. Through a combination of cognitive restructuring, behavioral interventions, and skills-building, CBT provides a comprehensive approach to address the multifaceted impact of trauma on thoughts, emotions, and behaviors.

5.2 Eye Movement Desensitization and Reprocessing (EMDR)

Eye Movement Desensitization and Reprocessing (EMDR) is a specialized therapeutic modality designed to alleviate the distress associated with traumatic memories. Developed by Francine Shapiro, EMDR has gained widespread recognition for its effectiveness in treating trauma-related disorders, including Complex PTSD.

EMDR incorporates a structured eight-phase approach, beginning with history-taking and treatment planning. One distinctive aspect of EMDR is the use of bilateral stimulation, typically achieved through the therapist guiding the client's eye movements. This bilateral stimulation is thought to facilitate the processing of traumatic memories, leading to desensitization and adaptive resolution.

In the initial phases of EMDR, therapists work collaboratively with clients to identify specific target memories related to the trauma. These memories are then processed using bilateral stimulation, with clients simultaneously focusing on associated thoughts, feelings, and physical sensations. The aim is to facilitate the adaptive processing of traumatic memories, allowing individuals to integrate these experiences into their overall narrative.

EMDR also incorporates elements of cognitive restructuring, as clients explore and challenge negative beliefs associated with traumatic memories. This dual-focus on both cognitive and sensory processing distinguishes EMDR as a comprehensive therapeutic approach for Complex PTSD.

One of the strengths of EMDR lies in its ability to access and process traumatic memories without requiring clients to provide extensive verbal details. This is particularly beneficial for individuals who may find traditional talk therapy challenging or retraumatizing. EMDR provides an avenue for processing traumatic memories while minimizing the risk of overwhelming emotional distress.

Additionally, EMDR recognizes the importance of fostering a sense of safety and containment throughout the therapeutic process. Clients are equipped with grounding techniques and coping strategies to manage any distress that may arise during or after EMDR sessions. This emphasis on ensuring the client's well-being aligns with the trauma-informed principles essential for effective treatment of Complex PTSD.

5.3 Dialectical Behavior Therapy (DBT)

Dialectical Behavior Therapy (DBT) is a therapeutic approach initially developed to treat individuals with borderline personality disorder, but it has shown efficacy in addressing the complex needs of trauma survivors, including those with Complex PTSD. Marsha M. Linehan, the creator of DBT, designed the approach to integrate cognitive-behavioral strategies with mindfulness and acceptance-based practices.

DBT operates on the principle of dialectics, acknowledging the inherent tension between acceptance and change. In the context of Complex PTSD, DBT helps individuals navigate the conflicting emotions and beliefs that often arise from traumatic experiences. The comprehensive nature of DBT addresses emotional dysregulation, interpersonal difficulties, and self-destructive behaviors commonly associated with trauma sequelae.

A central component of DBT is skills training, encompassing four modules: mindfulness, distress tolerance, emotion regulation, and interpersonal effectiveness. Mindfulness skills encourage individuals to stay present and non-judgmentally observe their thoughts and feelings, fostering a sense of self-awareness. Distress tolerance skills equip individuals with effective strategies to manage intense emotions without resorting to destructive behaviors.

Emotion regulation within DBT focuses on identifying and modulating intense emotional states. For survivors of Complex PTSD, this module provides valuable tools to navigate the unpredictable and overwhelming emotions often triggered by trauma-related stimuli. Learning to tolerate distressing emotions without resorting to avoidance or self-harm is a crucial aspect of this skill-building process.

Interpersonal effectiveness skills within DBT address challenges in forming and maintaining healthy relationships. Trauma survivors may grapple with issues of trust, boundary-setting, and effective communication. DBT provides practical strategies to navigate these interpersonal challenges, empowering individuals to build and sustain meaningful connections.

The acceptance and change dialectic within DBT encourages individuals to accept themselves and their current circumstances while simultaneously working towards positive change. This balance aligns with the nuanced needs of Complex PTSD, where acknowledging the impact of trauma coexists with a commitment to healing and growth.

DBT also incorporates a therapeutic component known as individual therapy, where clients work collaboratively with therapists to address specific challenges and develop personalized coping strategies. The therapeutic relationship within DBT is characterized by validation, support, and a commitment to dialectical synthesis.

PART III: OVERCOMING DISSOCIATIVE SYMPTOMS

Chapter 6

Grounding Techniques for Dissociation

Dissociation, a common response to overwhelming trauma, involves a disconnection from one's thoughts, feelings, or reality. Grounding techniques play a pivotal role in helping individuals regain a sense of connection and presence in the moment.

6.1 Mindfulness and Meditation

Mindfulness and meditation offer profound and accessible avenues for grounding individuals experiencing dissociation. Rooted in ancient contemplative practices, these techniques have gained significant recognition in modern therapeutic contexts, particularly for their effectiveness in managing stress, anxiety, and trauma-related symptoms.

Mindfulness involves cultivating present-moment awareness without judgment. For individuals experiencing dissociation, the practice of mindfulness provides a means to reconnect with the immediate sensations, thoughts, and emotions in a non-reactive manner. Mindfulness invites individuals to observe their internal experiences without becoming overwhelmed by them, fostering a sense of detachment from distressing thoughts or memories.

One fundamental aspect of mindfulness is conscious breathing. By directing attention to the breath – the rhythmic inhalation and exhalation – individuals can ground themselves in the physical sensations of the present moment. This simple yet powerful technique provides a focal point, helping to anchor the mind and alleviate the disconnection associated with dissociation.

Guided mindfulness meditations, often available in various forms such as audio recordings or meditation apps, offer structured support for individuals new to the practice. These guided sessions typically direct attention to specific sensations, sounds, or breath, providing a gentle and accessible introduction to mindfulness for those navigating dissociative experiences.

Meditation, an extension of mindfulness, encompasses a variety of practices designed to promote relaxation, concentration, and self-awareness. Visualization meditations, where individuals mentally focus on calming images or scenarios, can be particularly effective for grounding. This form of meditation engages the imagination to create a safe mental space, counteracting the dissociative tendencies that distance individuals from their immediate surroundings.

Body scan meditations are another valuable tool within the realm of meditation for grounding. This practice involves directing attention systematically through different parts of the body, heightening awareness of physical sensations. For those experiencing dissociation, the body scan can serve as an anchor, fostering connection with the corporeal self and grounding individuals in the present moment.

Mindfulness and meditation are not one-size-fits-all practices, and customization is key to their effectiveness. Tailoring these techniques to individual preferences and comfort levels ensures that they resonate with the unique needs of those managing dissociative symptoms. Regular practice cultivates a familiarity with grounding through mindfulness, empowering individuals to draw upon these techniques during moments of dissociation.

6.2 Sensory Grounding Exercises

Sensory grounding exercises leverage the power of the senses to reconnect individuals with their immediate environment, providing a tangible and effective approach to managing dissociation. These exercises engage the sensory experience, inviting individuals to anchor themselves through touch, sight, sound, taste, and smell.

One foundational sensory grounding technique is the 5-4-3-2-1 exercise. In this practice, individuals consciously engage their senses by identifying five things they can see, four things they can touch, three things they can hear, two things they can smell, and one thing they can taste. This structured approach directs attention outward, grounding individuals in the richness of their sensory surroundings.

Touch-based grounding exercises include activities such as holding onto a comforting object, feeling its texture, and focusing on the tactile sensations it provides. Squeezing a stress ball, running fingers through textured fabric, or holding a smooth stone can serve as tangible anchors, bridging the gap between dissociation and present awareness.

Visual grounding techniques leverage the sense of sight to bring individuals back to the present. This can involve focusing on a specific point in the environment, observing details in the surroundings, or engaging in activities that capture visual attention. Visualization exercises, where individuals mentally picture a serene or familiar place, offer a form of guided imagery that counteracts dissociation.

Auditory grounding exercises use the sense of hearing to create connection and presence. This may involve listening to calming music, nature sounds, or engaging in mindful listening where individuals intentionally focus on identifying and naming the sounds in their environment. The rhythmic nature of certain sounds can be particularly effective in grounding individuals.

Taste and smell, often powerful triggers of memory, can also be harnessed for grounding. Engaging in mindful eating, savoring the flavors of a simple food item, or utilizing scents such as essential oils can activate the sensory pathways associated with taste and smell, providing a direct connection to the present moment.

Combining multiple senses in a grounding exercise, such as holding a warm cup of tea while focusing on its aroma and taste, amplifies the sensory experience and enhances the grounding effect. The key is to engage the senses intentionally, creating a multisensory experience that interrupts dissociation and fosters a return to the present.

Customization is integral to the effectiveness of sensory grounding exercises. Individuals are encouraged to explore various sensory activities to identify those that resonate most with them. Incorporating these techniques into a daily routine builds familiarity, empowering individuals to employ them proactively during moments of dissociation and distress.

Chapter 7

Managing Flashbacks and Triggers

Trauma survivors often grapple with the distressing impact of flashbacks and triggers, pervasive elements of the post-traumatic experience.

7.1 Identifying Triggers

Triggers, stimuli that evoke intense emotional or physiological reactions linked to traumatic memories, are integral to understanding and managing the aftermath of trauma. Identifying triggers is a crucial step in the process of reclaiming agency over one's emotional and mental well-being. Triggers can manifest in various forms, including sensory cues, specific situations, or even certain individuals. Recognizing and acknowledging these triggers is foundational to developing effective coping mechanisms and minimizing the impact of flashbacks.

The identification of triggers often involves a collaborative exploration between individuals and their mental health professionals. Therapists, specializing in trauma-informed care, work alongside survivors to create a safe space where triggers can be openly discussed and identified. This process requires a delicate balance, as survivors navigate the potential reactivation of trauma-related emotions during trigger exploration.

Common triggers may include sensory stimuli reminiscent of the traumatic event, such as specific smells, sounds, or tactile sensations. Visual cues, such as scenes resembling the traumatic incident, can also trigger distressing memories. Situational triggers, such as crowded spaces, confined environments, or situations reminiscent of the traumatic event, can evoke a strong emotional response.

The identification of triggers extends beyond the external environment; internal triggers rooted in thoughts, emotions, or bodily sensations are equally significant. Intrusive thoughts, overwhelming emotions, or physiological sensations reminiscent of the trauma can serve as internal triggers, intensifying the vulnerability to flashbacks.

Journaling is a valuable tool in the process of identifying triggers. Encouraging individuals to maintain a trigger journal facilitates self-reflection and helps establish patterns related to specific triggers. Over time, this journal becomes a resource for individuals and their mental health professionals to collaboratively address and mitigate triggers during therapeutic interventions.

Self-awareness plays a pivotal role in trigger identification. Mindfulness practices, such as staying present and observing internal experiences without judgment, empower individuals to recognize triggers as they arise. The cultivation of mindfulness fosters a heightened sense of agency, allowing survivors to respond proactively to triggers rather than reactively.

Once triggers are identified, a collaborative effort between survivors and their support network is crucial. Loved ones, friends, and colleagues can contribute to a trauma-informed environment by understanding and respecting triggers. Open communication about triggers enables individuals to navigate social and interpersonal spaces with increased confidence and support.

It is essential to acknowledge that trigger identification is an ongoing and evolving process. As individuals progress in their recovery, new triggers may emerge, or existing triggers may lose their intensity. The flexibility to adapt and refine the understanding of triggers ensures a dynamic approach to managing the impact of trauma on daily life.

7.2 Coping Strategies for Flashbacks

Flashbacks, vivid and distressing recollections of traumatic events, can be debilitating for trauma survivors. Coping with flashbacks requires a multifaceted approach that addresses the immediate distress while also fostering resilience and a sense of safety.

One foundational coping strategy for flashbacks involves grounding techniques. Grounding brings individuals back to the present moment, interrupting the distressing narrative of the flashback. Techniques such as conscious breathing, where individuals focus on the rhythm of their breath, provide a tangible anchor in the midst of a flashback. Guided grounding exercises, incorporating sensory experiences, further enhance the effectiveness of grounding during flashbacks.

Creating a personalized "safety kit" is another proactive coping strategy. This kit may include comforting objects, soothing scents, or items with personal significance. Having this kit readily available allows individuals to access tangible sources of comfort during a flashback, promoting a sense of safety and stability.

Therapeutic interventions, such as Eye Movement Desensitization and Reprocessing (EMDR) or

Cognitive-Behavioral Therapy (CBT), are specifically designed to address and alleviate the impact of flashbacks. EMDR, in particular, involves guided bilateral stimulation to facilitate the processing and desensitization of traumatic memories. CBT incorporates cognitive restructuring to challenge and reframe negative thoughts associated with flashbacks.

Mindfulness practices play a transformative role in coping with flashbacks. Mindfulness invites individuals to observe the flashback without becoming entangled in its emotional grip. Mindful breathing and body scan exercises allow individuals to anchor themselves in the present, diminishing the intensity of the flashback. Mindfulness-based interventions, such as Mindfulness-Based Stress Reduction (MBSR), offer structured programs that teach individuals to integrate mindfulness into their daily lives.

Establishing a safety plan is a proactive coping strategy that empowers individuals to navigate flashbacks with a sense of control. This plan may involve identifying safe spaces, contacting a trusted support person, or engaging in specific grounding activities. Collaboratively developing a safety plan with mental health professionals ensures that it aligns with the unique needs and preferences of the individual.

Validation and self-compassion are integral components of coping with flashbacks. Recognizing that flashbacks are normal responses to abnormal experiences reduces self-blame and fosters self-compassion. Journaling can serve as a tool for self-reflection, allowing individuals to express and process their emotions during and after a flashback.

Engaging in creative pursuits can be a transformative coping strategy for flashbacks. Art, music, writing, or other forms of creative expression provide an outlet for individuals to channel their emotions constructively. Creativity becomes a means of reclaiming agency and transforming the narrative of the flashback into a form of personal expression and empowerment.

Peer support and group therapy offer a communal space for individuals to share their experiences and coping strategies. Connecting with others who have navigated similar challenges fosters a sense of understanding and shared resilience. Peer support groups create a community where individuals feel seen and validated, diminishing the isolation often associated with flashbacks.

Physical self-care, including activities such as exercise, proper nutrition, and sufficient sleep, contributes to overall well-being and resilience. Engaging in physical activities releases endorphins, which can counteract the physiological impact of flashbacks. Prioritizing physical self-care establishes a foundation for emotional and mental resilience.

In crisis situations, crisis helplines or text support services can provide immediate assistance. Having access to these resources ensures that individuals experiencing distressing flashbacks have a confidential and supportive outlet to seek help.

PART IV: REBUILDING AND THRIVING

Chapter 8

Reconnecting with the Self

Reconnecting with the self is a pivotal aspect of the recovery journey for individuals who have experienced trauma.

8.1 Developing a Positive Self-Image

Trauma often leaves an indelible mark on one's self-perception, giving rise to negative self-images and distorted beliefs. Developing a positive self-image is an essential step in the journey toward reconnecting with the self. This involves a deliberate and compassionate exploration of one's identity, strengths, and inherent worth, counteracting the damaging narratives that trauma can instill.

A key component of developing a positive self-image is the cultivation of self-compassion. Self-compassion involves treating oneself with kindness and understanding, particularly in the face of challenges and setbacks. Dr. Kristin Neff's research on self-compassion highlights its three core elements: self-kindness, common humanity, and mindfulness. Embracing self-kindness involves acknowledging and soothing oneself during difficult moments, recognizing that suffering is a shared human experience fosters a sense of common humanity, and approaching one's experiences with mindfulness allows for a non-judgmental awareness.

Therapeutic modalities, such as Compassion-Focused Therapy (CFT) and Acceptance and Commitment Therapy (ACT), offer structured approaches to cultivating self-compassion. CFT, developed by Dr. Paul Gilbert, focuses on developing an inner compassionate self that can counteract self-critical thoughts. ACT, on the other hand, emphasizes accepting uncomfortable thoughts and emotions while committing to values-aligned actions, promoting a sense of self-worth independent of immediate emotional states.

Positive affirmations play a role in challenging and reshaping negative self-talk. Affirmations are statements that affirm one's inherent worth, strengths, and capacity for growth. Consistent repetition of positive affirmations helps rewire neural pathways associated with negative self-perceptions, gradually replacing self-criticism with self-affirmation.

Reconnecting with the self also involves acknowledging and embracing one's strengths and achievements. The process of identifying personal strengths may involve reflection, self-assessment, and feedback from supportive individuals. Strengths-based approaches, common in positive psychology, encourage individuals to leverage their innate abilities and qualities as a foundation for growth and self-discovery.

Engaging in activities that bring joy and a sense of accomplishment contributes to the development of a positive self-image. Hobbies, creative pursuits, or pursuits aligned with personal interests provide opportunities for individuals to experience mastery, autonomy, and a positive sense of self. Recognizing and celebrating these achievements reinforces a positive self-perception.

Supportive relationships play a crucial role in shaping a positive self-image. Surrounding oneself with individuals who offer encouragement, validation, and empathy creates a social context that nurtures self-worth. Positive social interactions contribute to a sense of belonging, counteracting the isolation that often accompanies negative self-images.

Mindfulness practices, such as self-reflective journaling or mindful self-compassion exercises, deepen the connection with one's inner self. Mindfulness fosters a non-judgmental awareness of thoughts and feelings, allowing individuals to observe self-critical patterns and gently redirect their focus towards self-acceptance.

Challenging societal and cultural narratives that contribute to negative self-images is an empowering aspect of developing a positive self-image. Critical examination of societal expectations and stereotypes enables individuals to redefine success, beauty, and worth on their own terms. Advocacy for diverse and inclusive representations promotes a broader and more affirming understanding of human identity.

8.2 Rebuilding Trust in Yourself and Others

The aftermath of trauma often erodes trust – in oneself, others, and the world at large. Rebuilding trust is a transformative aspect of reconnecting with the self, requiring a deliberate and patient exploration of one's capacity to trust and be trusted. This process involves addressing the impact of betrayal, vulnerability, and the pervasive fear that accompanies trauma.

Rebuilding trust in oneself begins with recognizing and challenging self-doubt. Trauma can instill a deep sense of mistrust in one's own judgment, capabilities, and worthiness. Cognitive restructuring, a therapeutic technique within Cognitive-Behavioral Therapy (CBT), assists individuals in identifying and challenging negative self-beliefs. This involves examining evidence that contradicts self-doubt, recognizing personal strengths, and fostering a more balanced and self-affirming perspective.

Setting and achieving small, realistic goals is a foundational step in rebuilding trust in oneself. These goals serve as tangible evidence of one's capacity for agency and accomplishment. Celebrating these achievements, no matter how modest, reinforces a positive self-perception and gradually rebuilds a sense of self-trust.

Mindfulness practices contribute to rebuilding trust in oneself by promoting self-awareness and acceptance. Mindful self-compassion exercises, where individuals extend the same kindness and understanding to themselves as they would to a friend, foster a compassionate and non-judgmental relationship with one's inner self. Mindfulness also allows individuals to observe and redirect self-critical thoughts, promoting a more supportive and trusting internal dialogue.

Therapeutic interventions, such as trauma-focused therapies, provide a structured space for individuals to explore and process the roots of self-distrust. Trauma-focused Cognitive-Behavioral Therapy

(TF-CBT) and Internal Family Systems (IFS) therapy, for example, address the impact of trauma on self-perception and trust. These modalities provide tools for individuals to navigate internal conflicts, reframe self-narratives, and rebuild trust in their own capacity for growth and resilience.

Rebuilding trust in others involves a nuanced exploration of interpersonal dynamics. Trauma often instills a heightened sense of vulnerability and a fear of betrayal, making trust in relationships challenging. Setting healthy boundaries is an essential component of rebuilding trust in others. Clear and assertive communication about personal boundaries establishes a framework for safe and respectful interactions, allowing individuals to gradually rebuild trust in the reliability of these boundaries.

Social support plays a pivotal role in the process of rebuilding trust in others. Connecting with trustworthy individuals who demonstrate empathy, reliability, and understanding creates a foundation for rebuilding interpersonal trust. Supportive relationships provide opportunities for individuals to experience positive interactions, counteracting the mistrust that trauma may have engendered.

Group therapy or support groups offer a communal space where individuals can share their experiences, challenges, and successes in rebuilding trust. Connecting with others who have navigated similar journeys fosters a sense of shared understanding and validation, reducing the isolation that often accompanies trust issues.

Practicing forgiveness is a profound and empowering aspect of rebuilding trust in others. Forgiveness is not about condoning harmful actions but releasing the emotional burden associated with holding onto resentment. Forgiveness allows individuals to reclaim agency over their emotional well-being and create space for healing in relationships.

Rebuilding trust in the world involves confronting and challenging the pervasive fear that trauma can instill. This may involve gradually exposing oneself to situations that trigger fear and anxiety, employing gradual desensitization techniques within the framework of therapeutic interventions. Exposure therapy, a component of many trauma-focused therapies, provides a structured approach to facing feared situations in a controlled and supportive environment. The gradual and systematic exposure to triggers allows individuals to build resilience and challenge the overarching fear that the world is inherently unsafe.

Engaging in activities that promote a sense of safety and predictability contributes to rebuilding trust in the world.

Creating routines, establishing a supportive and predictable environment, and participating in activities that evoke positive emotions foster a perception of stability and control. These intentional choices provide a counterbalance to the chaotic and unpredictable nature of traumatic experiences.

Rebuilding trust in the world also involves critically examining and challenging distorted beliefs about safety and danger. Cognitive restructuring, a technique within Cognitive-Behavioral Therapy (CBT), addresses maladaptive thought patterns related to safety and threat. By exploring evidence that contradicts catastrophic beliefs and fostering a more realistic perspective, individuals gradually reshape their perception of the world.

Advocacy for social justice and collective healing can be a transformative avenue in rebuilding trust in the world. Participating in community initiatives, engaging in activism, or supporting causes aligned with values contribute to a sense of agency and connection. These efforts foster a belief in the potential for positive change, counteracting the disillusionment that may result from traumatic experiences.

Spirituality or a sense of connection to something greater than oneself can be a source of solace and support in rebuilding trust in the world. Engaging in spiritual practices, exploring existential questions, or participating in a faith community provides a framework for meaning-making and a sense of purpose.

Rebuilding trust is an ongoing and dynamic process that unfolds gradually. It requires patience, self-compassion, and a willingness to confront and challenge ingrained patterns of mistrust. Therapeutic support is instrumental in navigating the complexities of trust recovery, offering guidance, tools, and a safe space for exploration.

Chapter 9

Building Healthy Relationships

Building healthy relationships is a crucial aspect of the recovery journey for individuals who have experienced trauma.

9.1 Communication Skills in Relationships

Effective communication serves as the cornerstone of healthy relationships, playing a pivotal role in fostering understanding, trust, and emotional connection. For individuals navigating the aftermath of trauma, developing and honing communication skills is essential for establishing and maintaining relationships that provide support and resilience.

A fundamental aspect of communication skills is cultivating active listening. Active listening involves fully concentrating, understanding, responding, and remembering what is being said. Trauma survivors may carry a heightened sensitivity to communication nuances, making active listening an invaluable skill in creating a safe and validating space for open dialogue. Active listening fosters a sense of being heard and understood, essential elements in building trust within relationships.

Expressing oneself assertively is another key component of effective communication. Assertiveness involves communicating one's thoughts, feelings, and needs in a clear and respectful manner. Trauma survivors may grapple with assertiveness, having experienced powerlessness during traumatic events. Learning assertiveness skills empowers individuals to voice their boundaries, preferences, and concerns while fostering mutual respect within relationships.

Healthy communication also encompasses the ability to navigate conflict constructively. Conflict is a natural aspect of any relationship, and addressing it in a healthy manner is crucial for relationship growth. Trauma survivors may carry apprehensions about conflict due to past experiences, making it imperative to develop conflict resolution skills. These skills involve active listening, expressing emotions without blame, and collaboratively seeking solutions that meet the needs of all involved parties.

Setting and respecting boundaries is a foundational aspect of communication in relationships. Trauma can blur boundaries, leading to challenges in asserting and maintaining personal limits. Learning to establish clear and healthy boundaries ensures that individuals feel safe and respected within relationships. Boundaries provide a framework for mutual understanding and help prevent potential triggers or retraumatization.

Emotional regulation is intertwined with effective communication, especially for trauma survivors who may experience intense emotional reactions. Developing skills in recognizing, understanding, and managing emotions contributes to the ability to communicate calmly and thoughtfully. Mindfulness practices, such as grounding techniques and emotional awareness exercises, serve as valuable tools in enhancing emotional regulation.

Therapeutic interventions, including individual and couples therapy, offer a supportive environment for honing communication skills. Trauma-focused therapies may specifically address communication challenges stemming from past traumatic experiences. Couples therapy provides a collaborative space for partners to learn and practice effective communication techniques, fostering a deeper understanding of each other's needs and perspectives.

Cultivating empathy is essential in building healthy relationships, particularly for individuals with a history of trauma. Empathy involves understanding and sharing another person's feelings, creating a foundation of connection and mutual support. Trauma survivors may benefit from developing self-empathy as well, acknowledging and validating their own emotions and experiences.

9.2 Navigating Intimacy After Trauma

Intimacy, both emotional and physical, plays a vital role in the dynamics of romantic relationships. Navigating intimacy after trauma requires a nuanced and compassionate approach, considering the unique challenges and sensitivities that may arise for individuals who have experienced traumatic events.

For trauma survivors, the impact of past experiences on intimacy can be profound. The process of navigating intimacy involves understanding and addressing triggers, establishing clear communication, and prioritizing mutual consent and comfort.

Understanding and addressing triggers is an essential aspect of navigating intimacy after trauma. Triggers are stimuli that evoke distressing memories or emotional reactions related to traumatic experiences. Trauma survivors may experience triggers in intimate situations, potentially leading to anxiety, panic attacks, or dissociation. Open communication between partners about potential triggers and establishing a plan for managing them is crucial in creating a supportive and consensual intimate environment.

Creating a safe space for communication is fundamental in navigating intimacy after trauma. Partners should engage in open and honest conversations about boundaries, desires, and potential challenges. Establishing a sense of safety in expressing needs and concerns contributes to a more transparent and understanding intimate connection.

Consent is a cornerstone of healthy intimacy and becomes especially significant for trauma survivors. Prioritizing clear and enthusiastic consent ensures that both partners feel respected and comfortable in intimate situations. Establishing a mutual understanding of boundaries and regularly checking in with each other contributes to a consensual and empowering intimate relationship.

Therapeutic support is invaluable for individuals and couples navigating intimacy after trauma. Trauma-focused therapy can address the impact of past experiences on intimate relationships, providing tools and strategies for managing triggers and fostering emotional connection. Couples therapy offers a collaborative space for partners to explore and navigate the complexities of intimacy within the context of a supportive therapeutic relationship.

Gradual progression and pacing are key considerations in navigating physical intimacy after trauma. Partners should prioritize a pace that feels comfortable and consensual for both individuals. This may involve gradual exposure to physical touch, communication about preferences and comfort levels, and an ongoing dialogue to ensure a shared understanding of each other's needs.

Mindfulness practices, such as body awareness exercises and sensory grounding, can be beneficial in navigating physical intimacy. These practices allow individuals to stay present in the moment, fostering a connection with their own bodies and the sensations experienced during intimate encounters. Mindfulness also supports emotional regulation, reducing the likelihood of overwhelming emotional reactions during intimate moments.

Building emotional intimacy is a parallel process in navigating intimacy after trauma. Emotional intimacy involves sharing thoughts, feelings, and vulnerabilities with a partner, creating a deeper connection beyond the physical. Trauma survivors may benefit from developing trust and emotional closeness before engaging in physical intimacy, allowing for a more secure and consensual experience.

Exploring alternative forms of intimacy beyond traditional expectations can be empowering for trauma survivors. Intimacy is a diverse and multifaceted concept that extends beyond physical connection. Engaging in activities that promote emotional closeness, such as shared hobbies, deep conversations, or acts of kindness, contributes to the overall intimacy within a relationship.

Self-compassion is paramount for individuals navigating intimacy after trauma. Acknowledging and validating one's own experiences, setting realistic expectations, and prioritizing self-care contribute to a positive and empowered approach to intimacy. Self-compassion also involves recognizing and challenging any internalized shame or guilt related to past traumatic experiences.

Chapter 10

Pursuing a Path to Thriving

Thriving after trauma is not only about surviving but about reclaiming a sense of agency, purpose, and fulfillment.

10.1 Setting and Achieving Personal Goals

Setting and achieving personal goals is a transformative aspect of the recovery journey, offering individuals a sense of direction, purpose, and agency. For trauma survivors, intentional goal-setting becomes a powerful tool in reclaiming control over their lives and creating a roadmap towards a thriving future.

The process of setting personal goals begins with self-reflection and a deep understanding of one's values, desires, and aspirations. Trauma can disrupt a person's sense of identity and purpose, making the exploration of personal goals an opportunity for rediscovery. It involves asking fundamental questions about what brings meaning and fulfillment, both in the short and long term.

Incorporating the SMART criteria—Specific, Measurable, Achievable, Relevant, and Time-bound—enhances the effectiveness of goal-setting. Specific goals provide clarity on what is to be achieved, measurable criteria allow for tracking progress, achievable goals set realistic expectations, relevant goals align with personal values, and time-bound goals establish a timeframe for accomplishment.

Short-term and long-term goals play complementary roles in the recovery process. Short-term goals provide immediate direction and a sense of accomplishment, fostering motivation and confidence. Long-term goals offer a broader vision for the future, anchoring individuals in their overarching aspirations and contributing to a sustained sense of purpose.

Goal-setting is an inherently personal process, and the nature of goals varies widely among individuals. Some may focus on rebuilding social connections, pursuing education or career advancement, cultivating hobbies, or prioritizing self-care. The diversity of goals reflects the unique paths individuals take in their pursuit of thriving.

Therapeutic support can significantly enhance the goal-setting process. Mental health professionals, particularly those specializing in trauma-informed care, collaborate with individuals to explore and define meaningful goals. Therapy provides a supportive space for addressing potential barriers, navigating setbacks, and adjusting goals as individuals progress in their recovery.

The concept of post-traumatic growth emphasizes that adversity can be a catalyst for personal development and positive change. Setting goals aligned with post-traumatic growth involves framing challenges as opportunities for learning and resilience. This perspective encourages individuals to view their recovery journey not only as a response to trauma but as a transformative process that can lead to newfound strengths and capacities.

Achieving personal goals involves a combination of perseverance, self-compassion, and adaptability. The recovery journey is non-linear, and setbacks are inherent. Developing resilience in the face of obstacles and practicing self-compassion during challenging times are essential components of the goal achievement process.

Celebrating each step towards goal attainment is equally significant. Acknowledging progress, no matter how small, reinforces a positive and empowered mindset. This celebration not only boosts motivation but also cultivates a sense of self-efficacy—a belief in one's ability to overcome challenges and achieve desired outcomes.

10.2 Celebrating Milestones in Recovery

Celebrating milestones in recovery is an integral aspect of recognizing progress, cultivating resilience, and fostering a positive perspective on the journey towards thriving. Whether small victories or significant achievements, milestones represent moments of triumph, resilience, and growth for individuals who have experienced trauma. This section explores the importance of acknowledging and celebrating these milestones as part of the recovery process.

Milestones in recovery encompass a diverse range of achievements, both tangible and intangible. They may include overcoming a specific fear, successfully navigating a triggering situation, reaching a certain point in therapy, rebuilding a broken relationship, or making progress towards a personal goal. The significance of milestones lies not only in their outcome but in the resilience and effort that individuals invest in reaching them.

Acknowledging milestones contributes to the cultivation of a positive mindset and a sense of accomplishment. Trauma can often overshadow personal strengths and resilience, leading individuals to downplay their achievements. Celebrating milestones involves intentionally recognizing and honoring progress, creating a narrative of success and empowerment that counteracts the narrative of victimhood that may accompany traumatic experiences.

Validation from oneself and others is a key element in the milestone celebration process. Self-validation involves acknowledging the effort, courage, and growth that went into reaching a milestone. This internal acknowledgment is foundational in building self-esteem and fostering a positive self-image. External validation, whether from friends, family, or mental health professionals, reinforces the importance of the achieved milestone in the eyes of those who provide support.

Creating a ritual or symbolic gesture to mark a milestone adds a tangible and memorable dimension to the celebration. This could involve writing a letter to oneself, creating a piece of art, getting a symbolic tattoo, or engaging in a meaningful activity. Rituals provide a sense of closure, a visual reminder of progress, and a connection to the significance of the achieved milestone.

The concept of post-traumatic growth is particularly relevant in the context of celebrating milestones. Post-traumatic growth suggests that individuals can experience positive psychological changes as a result of struggling with and adapting to adversity. Recognizing and celebrating milestones aligns with this concept by emphasizing the transformative potential embedded within the recovery journey.

Group celebrations, such as support group gatherings or sharing achievements with a trusted community, offer a communal space for acknowledgment and encouragement. Connecting with others who have faced similar challenges fosters a sense of shared resilience and reinforces that milestones are not solitary achievements but collective triumphs within a supportive network.

Therapeutic support plays a crucial role in milestone celebration by providing a structured space to reflect on achievements and set new goals. Mental health professionals guide individuals in recognizing the significance of milestones, exploring the emotions associated with them, and integrating the positive aspects of progress into the overall narrative of recovery.

Navigating setbacks and acknowledging the ebb and flow of the recovery journey is an essential aspect of milestone celebration. Setbacks are inevitable, and resilience lies in the ability to learn from challenges, adjust strategies, and continue moving forward.

Celebrating milestones during setbacks involves recognizing the persistence and courage demonstrated in the face of adversity.

www.ingramcontent.com/pod-product-compliance
Lightning Source LLC
Chambersburg PA
CBHW050851260726

48660CB00006B/2566